My Baby [illegible]er Ned

written and illustrated by

Sumiko

CORGI BOOKS
A DIVISION OF TRANSWORLD PUBLISHERS LTD.

MY BABY BROTHER NED
A PICTURE CORGI 0 552 522929

PRINTING HISTORY
First published in 1981 by William Heinemann Ltd.
Corgi edition published 1985

Corgi Books are published by
Transworld Publishers Ltd.,
Century House, 61–63 Uxbridge Road,
Ealing, London W5 5SA

Printed and bound in Portugal by Printer Portuguesa

This book was designed with the help of the National Childbirth Trust and written in consultation with their Education Officer, Sue Dale Tunnicliffe, to help parents and young children talk about the arrival of a new baby in the family.

I have a baby brother.
His name is Ned.
Every day I help Mummy and Daddy
to look after him.

I wake up early in the morning.
Ned is still sleeping in his cot.
Mummy is asleep too.

Ned is awake now.
He smiles at me.
I like him smiling.

Ned can't talk yet.
He tells us what he wants
with his cries.
I think he is hungry now.

Mummy gives her milk to Ned.
He likes it very much.

I have cereal for breakfast
like Daddy and Mummy.
I crunch it with my teeth.
Ned hasn't any teeth yet.

Ned is too small to sit on a potty,
so he wears a nappy.
We have to change it often.
I can sit up on the lavatory
if I have a step.

Mummy and Daddy are
dressing Ned and me.
I can nearly dress myself,
but I can't do my buttons yet,
or do up my shoes.

When Daddy goes out,
Mummy does the washing.
I am good at helping her.

Ned lies in his pram. He watches the sun dancing on the leaves. Then he falls asleep.

I go out shopping with Mummy and Ned. I have a special seat on his pram.

On the way back I ride my bike.
People smile at Ned,
but they don't always talk to me.

Mummy makes our dinner.
Ned has had his milk.
He watches us and bangs his spoon.

Ned is asleep again.
He sleeps a lot.

Mummy is resting.
I play with my toys on the floor.

When Ned wakes up we play together.
I show him all the toys.
He likes his rattle best.
He sucks it and shakes it
to make a noise.

Ned snatches my book from me
and tears the pages. Oh Ned!
I get angry and cry.

Mummy cuddles us both.
"You must be careful what Ned
plays with," she says.

After tea we have our bath.
Daddy washes me, then I play
with my bath toys.

Ned laughs a lot in the water.
I help Mummy to wash him.

Sometimes I hold Ned.
He smells nice.
Daddy says I used to be
a baby like Ned.
Even Daddy and Mummy
were babies once.

It is Ned's bedtime.
Mummy tucks him into his cot.

Mummy and Daddy read me a story. They cuddle me and give me goodnight kisses.

I give Ned a kiss too,
and say goodnight to him.
I like my baby brother Ned.